DR. BELL'S

SYSTEM OF INSTRUCTION

BROKEN INTO

SHORT QUESTIONS AND ANSWERS

FOR THE

USE OF MASTERS AND TEACHERS

IN THE

NATIONAL SCHOOLS.

COMPILED AND ARRANGED BY THE

REV. FREDERIC IREMONGER, A.M. F.L.S.

SECRETARY TO THE HAMPSHIRE SOCIETY FOR THE
EDUCATION OF THE POOR.

London:

PRINTED FOR F. C. AND J. RIVINGTON,
Booksellers to the Society for Promoting Christian Knowledge,
NO. 62, ST. PAUL'S CHURCH-YARD;
By R. & R. Gilbert, St. John's Square, Clerkenwell.

1818.

ADVERTISEMENT.

In the following Tract, it is proper to state that there is not the most distant idea of superseding Dr. Bell's valuable publications, which cannot be too accurately, or too often perused, and which detail so fully the progress of his interesting Discovery ; still as the catechetical form of going through his System has been always found calculated to facilitate the instruction of persons who are learning it, and also to be of considerable use for the Masters of Central Schools, in examining those who are sent to them for this purpose, it was thought a work of this description would have many and important advantages in forwarding the great objects of the National Society for the Education of the Poor. It is believed that the latest improvements which have been adopted in the subsidiary practices of Dr. Bell's plan, are inserted in the present work. Should any slight variations, however, still be found in the mechanical part of the System, as it is here stated, and as it is practised at the National School, Baldwin's Gardens, they may easily be traced, by a reference to the last edition of Dr. Bell's Instructions for conducting Schools, while the leading principles must always remain unaltered, and have been, whenever fairly tried, eminently successful.

QUESTIONS AND ANSWERS

ON

DR. BELL'S

SYSTEM OF EDUCATION.

———

Question. WHAT is the first thing to be done in forming a School on the Madras, or Dr. Bell's System?

Answer. It is to be arranged into classes.

Q. By what method?

A. By dividing the children according to the knowledge they may have of reading, spelling, or their letters.

Q. How is the master to discover this?

A. By finding out who have been at the same school previously together, and what proficiency they have made, or if the number is small, he may examine them all himself.

Q. Of what number should the classes consist?

A. The best number is from 24 to 36, or in large schools to 40; but that is not always possible; 120 scholars may perhaps be divided into six classes, having respect, as near as may be, to equality of progress in forming each class.

Q. What is the next step ?

A. To select teachers, that is, the officers and agents, from among the children themselves, who are to assist in the government and instruction of the school.

Q. From what classes are the teachers selected ?

A. From the higher classes.

Q. How are they selected ?

A. By the elective voices of the higher classes, and best boys in the school, who scarcely ever fail to find the boys most suited for the purpose. A short time will enable the master to discover whether a right choice has been made. He must change them till he has good ones. They are to be found, and on the choice of these teachers the whole will depend.

Q. How should the master instruct the teachers in their duty ?

A. By getting them to attend him at first at extra hours.

Q. What should be the general character of the teachers ?

A. They must not merely be forward in their learning, but they must be boys of activity and energy, of good temper, steady to one thing ; of as much judgment and discrimination as you can expect at so young an age.

Q. What is the business of a teacher ?

A. To hear his class their lessons ; to keep the registers ; to apportion the length of each lesson, unless it is before determined by the regular rules of the school. In short, under the eye of the master, to direct the whole proceedings of the class; for the order, behaviour, and improvement of which he must be responsible.

Q. What else is also considered the business of the teacher?

A. He is expected, in particular, to tell, whenever asked, the number in his class both present and absent, the number of lessons said, and how much time has been occupied in saying them.

Q. What other officer is appointed to each class?

A. An assistant teacher.

Q. How is he selected?

A. From a higher class, or the best boy in each class, as circumstances may point out, or as the class may require particular attention.

Q. What is his business?

A. To assist the teacher in hearing the lessons, and in keeping order in the class; and in case of the teacher's absence, to take the whole management of it himself. Whenever the teacher leaves the class, if but for a moment, the assistant should take his office, and the head boy of the class that of the assistant.

Q. Who is placed over the teachers?

A. An usher, who is to be the most active and intelligent boy in the school. His business is to see that the teachers do their duty, to instruct them in it, if necessary; to see that the registers are rightly kept, and, in short, to issue, and to see executed, all the orders of the master.

Q. What is the duty of the master?

A. His perpetual employment is to overlook the whole school, and give life and energy to every member of it. He inspects the classes one by one, and is occupied, wherever there is most occasion for his services, and where they will have the greatest effect. He is to encourage the diffident, the timid, and the backward; to check and repress the forward and presumptuous, to bestow just and ample commendation upon the diligent, attentive, and orderly, however dull their capacity, or slow their progress; to regulate the ambitious, rouse the slothful, and make the idle exert themselves; in short, to deal out praise and blame, encouragement and threatening, according to the temper, disposition, and genius of the scholar. He is occasionally to hear and instruct the classes himself, and far oftener to watch over the general order, seeing that his numerous agents are at their posts, and alert, (rather than acting himself,) and overlooking the teachers and assistants, while hearing their respective classes.

Q. To whom is the master accountable?

A. To the superintendants, or visitors; one or more of whom, appointed every week, should attend the weekly examination, and as much oftener as they can make it convenient, and to them should all appeals be made. They should also make themselves thoroughly acquainted with the mechanical part of the system, in order that they may know whether it is accurately followed up, in all its parts, and whether the whole business of the School is conducted with order, method, and regularity.

Q. Having thus arranged the School, what should be the next object of the master?

A. If the size of the room will admit, to take care that each child has his standing room.

Q. If the room will admit, what space should each child occupy, when standing in his class?

A. About 16 or 18 inches.

Q. How should the places for the respective classes be distinguished?

A. They should be chalked or painted, so that they can always be seen, and the lines also chalked in front for the teacher and assistant teacher; " T" being written in chalk to signify the former, " A" the latter.

Q. Where should the writing desks be placed?

A. Close to the wall in that part of the room where there is most light.

Q. What number are necessary?

A. There need not be more than enough for one or at most two classes to write at a time.

Q. How should the rest of the space be managed?

A. The middle space of the room should be left clear, and on one side of the room, the forms may be placed in three rows, one behind the other, whenever the classes have occasion to sit down.

Q. What is particularly to be attended to in the arrangement of the classes?

A. That the whole of the classes, whether standing, sitting, or at prayers, should be so arranged, that the master may command the whole at one view.

Q. What is the simple principle, on which Dr. Bell's System rests?

A. Tuition by the scholars themselves.

Q. In saying their lessons to the teachers, how do the classes proceed?

A. The boy who prompts another, or tells him what he mistakes, takes his place, or precedence, in the class above him so prompted, and those between them. In taking the place, he always goes up in the front, and not in the rear, of him whom he corrects.

Q. What plan is pursued to fix the attention of the children?

A. In whatever part of the class a want of it may appear, the boy who is perceived to be inattentive is called upon to proceed; and if he hesitates, he loses his place.

Q. If a scholar grossly fails, or misbehaves himself what is to be done?

A. He is turned to the bottom of his class.

Q. When a scholar does not read audibly and distinctly, as often happens in the outset, or pronounces badly, or makes any of those mistakes which generally require a length of time to correct, what is to be done?

A. Each of the scholars under him, who reads audibly, &c. takes his place, till he either corrects himself, or sinks below all who do correct him.

Q. When a boy has held a high rank in his class for some time, what would you do with him ?

A. He may be either made assistant teacher of the class, or advanced to a superior class, where he is placed at the foot ; and if in a few days he rises near the middle, he maintains a permanent footing in this class ; if not, he must return to his original class.

Q. If a boy fails in saying his daily lesson, what is to be done ?

A. He is degraded to an inferior class, and placed at the head : and if he sinks to its level, he forfeits his former class.

Q. But if he maintains a high rank in this class, is he still to continue in the class to which he has been degraded ?

A. No ; he will be allowed to join his original class upon a new trial, when it often happens, that by redoubled exertion, he can now keep pace with the rest of the children in it.

Q. Is this method of change attended with any particular benefit ?

A. Yes. By these means no class is ever retarded, or kept back in its progress, by idle or dull boys ; and every boy, while he thus finds his own level in the school, is fully and profitably employed.

Q. What are the two general laws by which a school, on Dr. Bell's System, is conducted ?

A. 1. That every scholar is allowed, by a fair and constant competition with his fellows, to find his level.

2. That the instruction of the school is carried on by short, easy, continued, and perfect lessons.

Q. Should the master hesitate to unite two small classes into one ?

A. No. For advantage will be derived to the superior class from going over the ground again with the inferior class, and at all times the fewer the classes the better.

Q. What may be done with the teachers who are advanced considerably beyond the class of which they have the charge?

A: The master may give them books and tasks to learn at home, and thus enable them to carry on their own studies, at leisure hours, in the way which will be most advantageous to themselves, without interfering with the discharge of their office.

Q. What other plan may be adopted of advantage to the teachers and assistant teachers in their learning?

A. They should always, in their turn, read a portion of the lesson with their class.

Q. Can you point out any other way by which the teachers may be improved?

A. By having attention paid to them by the master for half an hour occasionally, when the other children are dismissed; and also by their going sometimes, for a short period of the day, into the first class, while the assistant teachers take the duty of the teachers in the respective classes.

Q. To whom should the master give his orders or instructions?

A. To the usher.

Q. And to whom should he deliver them?

A. To the teachers, and by the teachers to their respective classes.

Q. What is the advantage of this method?

A. One intelligent boy made to comprehend any thing in which there is the least difficulty, can bring it down to the level of his school-fellows capacity, and explain it to them far better than the master himself.

Q. What is the error most fatal to the well-being of a school, and to which the master is most liable?

A. Looking after individuals, and individual points, instead of seeing that his numerous officers are alert and active, and perform properly the respective offices allotted to them.

Q. If a teacher, or assistant teacher, does not report the misconduct of his class to the master, what is done?

A. He is himself reported for neglect by the usher; and if the usher should in like manner fail, he is in like manner answerable.

Q. If one part of a class is more imperfect than another, how may this be remedied?

A. The boys most backward may individually say their lessons to the more forward, i. e. they may be divided into tutor and pupil, and the former is responsible for the progress of the latter.

Q. What is the ground-work of all precision, and never dispensed with, without giving rise to much error and neglect?

A. The marked book.

Q. To whom are the marked books confined?

A. To the teachers and assistant teachers.

Q. Who should preserve a copy of them?

A. The master.

Q. For what purpose?

A. For the inspection of the superintendants and visitors.

Q. What is the duty of the master with regard to the marked book?

Q. In each class the master marks with pen and ink in the front of the teacher's book, when taken in hand, the number of the class, the teacher's name, the day of the month, the manner in which it is to be read, and whether for the first or second time, &c.

Q. What is the teacher's part in keeping the marked book?

A. The teacher marks with pencil the day of the month, at the place where the lesson begins, every morning, and also where each successive lesson during the day, as it is given out, ends.

Q. At the close of the school for the day, what is done?

A. The individual proficiency of each scholar, or the place which he holds in his class, and his absence from school, if that should happen, is entered in a register by the teachers, ushers, and other competent officers.

Q. What other register is kept?

A. The register of business, in which is inserted the sum of the daily tasks noted in the marked book, or performed during the day; the number of lessons read, pages or lines ended at, and hours thus employed, in three adjoining columns; and so with the catechism, religious instruction, writing, ciphering, &c. These are added weekly and monthly, and compared by the master and teachers with what was done the preceding day, week, and month.

Q. Of what particular benefit are the registers?

A. They are great instruments of discipline, and produce precision and exactness. Both to the master and visitor they afford the readiest means of ascertaining the progress and present state of the school, and the regularity of attendance of each scholar. It is at one view thus shewn what has been done during any given period by each class, and a trial will prove whether it has been gone over properly and correctly.

N. B. In Sunday Schools the register may be examined once in every month, and the progress of the children may be enquired into at any given period. This account should be kept by the masters of the schools at extra hours, as the time is limited when the school is held on Sundays alone. The process of instruction may be the same, but it would perhaps be advisable to have what is usually called, " the religious instruction," in the morning, and the reading in the afternoon.

Q. What mode would you take periodically to ascertain the progress of the children?

A. A weekly examination attended by the visitors and members of the Committee.

Q. In what way should such weekly examinations be conducted?

A. Each class should be brought up separately, and the teacher be desired to hear them, under the direction of the visitor in the whole of the preceding week's business, or such part of it as the visitor may think proper, or out of any books they have previously gone through.

Q. What particular advantage is there in directing the teacher to hear the classes at the examination?

A. The visitor will thus be enabled to ascertain whether the teacher is competent to his duty, and at the same time confidence will be given to the teacher, and what is very necessary, consequence, in the eyes of the class: the master should attend the class during the whole of the examination.

Q. What other useful office may the visitor undertake?

A. He may communicate any religious instruction, or explanation, of what the children are reading, and by easy questions he will see whether they comprehend what they read. Places should invariably be taken according to superiority in answering.

Q. As this system so much depends on the teachers of each class, what should be done to secure their exertions?

A. The forfeiture of the office through misconduct should be severely felt; and merit-tickets, prize-books, prize-medals, or any other kind of encouragement, may be given them, if their class is in such order, and makes such improvement as it ought to do.

Q. What reward may be given to the best children at the weekly examination?

A. Printed tickets of merit, of different value, some 6 for 6d. 4d. 2d. and so on according to their rank in the school; they may be paid at the time, or the account be set in the fund-book.

Q. What is the fund-book?

A. A book in which an account is kept of the number of tickets of merit due to the children, and the value of them; which value is given to such child, sometimes at the weekly, or other examination; or, it is suffered to accumulate till it can be applied to some useful purpose, or till the child quits the school.

Q. How would you discover who had made the most progress in each class, during the week?

A. I would find out who, on the whole, had been highest in the class, by examining the register for ascertaining individual progress, as it is called, in which the place each boy holds in his class, is noted down, and, of course, the boy, whose total number is the least, must have kept his rank highest, and he is placed first the beginning of the ensuing week, and so on through the class.

Q. In what proportion may the tickets be bestowed?

A. On the two first boys, according to the above plan, one each, and two to the teacher, if his class perform its examination to the satisfaction of the visitors.

Q. Is the register for ascertaining individual progress of any other use?

A. Yes. It proves what boy is absent each day, morning and afternoon. A. is affixed to his name, if absent without leave; and L. if with leave; S. if sick.

Q. How would you punish the absentees?

A. If they only come too late, by keeping them the same portion of time after their school-fellows are gone home. If absent a whole morning or evening, then by confinement and imposition, unless a satisfactory reason for non-attendance be sent to the master by the parent.

Q. How is the alphabet first taught?

A. By writing on sand and slates, and from cards.

Q. How is the writing on sand taught?

A. For this purpose, smooth and level trays, or boards, about three feet long, ten inches wide, with ledges on every side, of an inch deep (inside measurement) placed on a convenient bench or form, may each of them serve for three children. A little dry sand is put into them, so that with a shake it will become level, and spread itself thinly over the surface.

Q. What does the teacher then do?

A. He traces in the sand with his fore-finger a capital letter, of which there is a copy before him. The scholar traces the impression again and again, the teacher guiding his finger at first, if necessary, and the sand is then smoothed with a shake.

Q. What is next done?

A. The scholar, looking at the letter before him, tries to copy it, and is assisted as before, and directed till he can do it with ease and with precision. The copy is then withdrawn, and the scholar must now form it from memory.

Q. What follows after one letter has been thus taught?

A. In like manner a second letter is thus taught; he then returns to the former, and makes alternately the one and the other, till he can form both with readiness and exactness. This done, he proceeds to a third, and so on, never taking in hand a letter till he is familiar with all that precede it.

Q. How may the letters be printed for this purpose?

A. The letters (large and small) may be printed on a sheet of paper, then cut out separately, and put on pasteboard. (This will make them last some time; three alphabets done in this manner will suffice.)

Q. What letters should be first chosen?

A. The capitals, I, L, T, O.

Q. To what other letters should particular attention be shewn?

A. b, d, p, q.

Q. How is the pupil taught to distinguish them?

A. By telling him that each is formed of an o, and a straight line; that the o, in b and p, is on the right, and in d and q, on the left; or by such other device as will readily occur to the earnest teacher.

Q. What else may be taught by writing on sand?

A. The double letters, digits, numerals, and stops.

Q. Having finished with the sand and slate, (and the writing the alphabet on slates, is perhaps the best plan) how is the alphabet now read?

A. On the first leaf of the First Book of the National Society.

Q. After leaving the alphabet, how are pages 3 and 4, of the monosyllabic cards, or National Society School Book, No. 1, begun?

A. By what is termed a loud or repeating lesson.

Q. Of what quantity do the first lessons consist?

A. The words, " page 3," compose the first of these repeating lessons; afterwards the two first words; and then the last three in the first line.

Q. What is the manner of saying the " repeating lesson?"

A. The teacher gives out the words or letters himself, and then the whole class are to follow him by a loud, slow, and distinct pronunciation.

Q. How is this done? State the plan more particularly.

A. The teacher says "Page." The whole class immediately and together say the same. Then the teacher, "3;" class "3." Then the teacher, "1;" the class "1." Teacher, "a;" class, "a." Teacher, "la;" class, "la." The assistant teacher gives it out next in the same way, each boy following as before, and then every child in the class in turn.

Q. What is next taught?

A. The following word, "le."

Q. Is this taught in the same manner?

A. Yes. It is repeated backward and forward, first by the teacher, then the assistant teacher, then each one in the class as before; and then the three following words form the next lesson also in the same manner.

Q. How long are the repeating lessons continued?

A. Generally one line will be sufficient; but they should be continued till the class has obtained a distinct and steady mode of pronouncing the letters, and till their attention is so far fixed, that they will read the letters themselves, as they follow in the succession of words on the cards.

Q. How does the class then proceed?

A. Forming the letters into syllables, each child taking a letter, reading the card across, and taking three, four, or five syllables for a lesson, according to their proficiency; though the children ought soon to be able to learn one line at a lesson.

Q. What should the teacher invariably say, when he thinks the lesson is of a proper length?

A. "Stop;" or else, give some sign which the children will understand.

Q. What is then done?

A. Then the lesson is read in the way just mentioned,

first " backwards," after " stop" has been said; then forwards and backwards, backwards and forwards, (beginning with any child indiscriminately) till the teacher says, " Shut books;" or, when the school is numerous, makes a sign.

- Q. What are the scholars then called upon to do?

A. The teacher makes them spell the words off book, beginning always with the hardest word in the lesson.

Q. How are the scholars taught to spell the syllables?

A. *On* book, thus: l-a, la. *Off* book, la, l-a.

Q. What is this called?

A. Previous spelling.

Q. How often must each card be thus read by previous spelling?

A. Two or three times, if necessary; or only once if the class is perfect in the whole, when examined in any and every part of it.

Q. After previous spelling, in what way is each card or leaf (which is considered as a distinct book) gone through?

A. Word by word, thus: " la," " le," &c.

Q. What quantity is generally learnt for each lesson?

A. The first time of going over the cards in either of these ways, i. e. by previous spelling, or word by word, one line is in general learnt, and two lines the second time.

Q. In what manner are places taken?

A. The child who corrects another, or sets him right in any mistake he has made, goes above him, in front; the child who loses a place, goes down behind the other. The child that is prompted, or set right, should go down before he corrects himself.

Q. Is it desirable for the children to go to their seats in order to get their lessons?

A. No. For by spending the time allowed them to get

it, in saying it to their teachers, they will learn it more effectually. At least the class need only go to their seats once in five or six lessons; and if recreation is necessary, it may be better done by the children going for a few minutes into their yard or play-ground.

Q. When a scholar, who has made some progress, comes to school, with what does he begin?

A. Generally with the sand-board, or lowest class, and he works his way up so as to find his level; but this may be left to the discretion of the master.

Q. How should a fresh class, which has made some progress in other schools, be taught the new mode of saying lessons?

A. By each of the scholars reading in the alphabet, or monosyllables, with which they are acquainted, a short lesson, in which case, thirty, and even sixty, lessons have been said in an hour.

Q. At what period is previous spelling discontinued?

A. When the Monosyllabic Spelling-book is finished.

Q. Is there no exception to this rule?

A. Yes. If after all that has been done, the scholar meets with a syllable which puzzles him, he divides that syllable, and that only into letters, by previous spelling, to enable him to read it.

Q. How are the children taught to turn to any place in their book?

A. They are taught to do so by degrees, and almost insensibly, by never passing a page or verse, or chapter or lesson, without reading or learning its number.

Q. When are the stops or points learnt?

A. At the end of the monosyllabic cards; and they are taught on the sand, the same as the letters, what each stop is, and how long the reader should pause at it in reading.

Q. How are the children practised in the use of the stops?

A. By the teacher asking the child in the class, who may be reading, what the stop is? what is the proper pause to be made? and desiring the class to make a resemblance of it with the finger on the book.

Q. How is attention to this essential point afterwards secured?

A. By taking places. Any child correcting another for not attending properly to the stops, gets above the one so offending.

Q. How may particular attention be gained to the hardest words?

A. By asking what renders any particular word difficult. Thus: Why is " phlegm" a difficult word? Because the g is not sounded, and because the p h sounds like f. " Dream?" ea sounds like ee, double e. " Wretch?" The w is not sounded.

Q. What is the new way in which the alphabet is taught at the National School?

A. First tutor from a higher class makes pupil in the lowest class write letter I, exactly like a copy placed before the child, with one stroke; the letter L in the same way, and the same distance; then I and L alternately; then T and O in the same way; then I, L, T, O. Then form a class; and let the children read this lesson off their slate, in a card lesson, counting six between each letter; the class all repeating with the teacher aloud, the same as a loud or repeating lesson. Next, each child reads the whole lesson, counting six between, in a low voice; then each one takes a letter, counting as before. Then leave slates, and write by dictation promiscuously. Then read from slates, each taking a letter. The whole alphabet is taught in this manner.

Q. Does this apply to the *printed* and written characters?

A. The writing of the printed characters is comparatively of small moment, and the reading of them is almost insensibly acquired, when the written letters are known.

Q. What is the manner in which, according to this new plan of learning to write and read at the same time, the cards are gone through ?

A. When the alphabet is finished, and the class begins, page 3, the page is given out by a child, saying, page, next 3, till perfect. Then 3 is written in the slate corner. The slate is then put over the book, so that still the lesson may be seen. Child says " l," the children all write " l;" next says " a," all write " a;" next says " la," and so on to the end of the line. The teacher says, " Stop. "Then the books are hid. Then read lesson backwards, by previous spelling if necessary from slate, and forwards till teacher gives a signal ; then read it by words till perfect ; or at once by words, then turn slates by signal, and write promiscuously by dictation. Teacher says " la ;" the child, whose turn it is to begin, says " la" after him ; the next " l," all write " l;" next " a," all write " a." The lesson when all the words are thus written, is read over by words once.

Q. How long is this continued ?

A. To the end of page 8.

Q. How are the cards from p. 9 to p. 12 learnt?

A. By the children sitting down, and writing for half an hour, or an hour, each day, in the following manner : The teacher says " spar," all write " spar," looking on the cards ; each word is done in this way, and two, three, or even four lines may be given for a lesson. Then the teacher says " stop," the cards are hid, the lesson is read backwards and forwards by words from the slate several times, the children whispering each word, as the child, whose turn it is, says it aloud. When perfect in this manner, the lesson is spelt as before, and read once by words backwards.

Q. While the spelling cards from p. 9 to p. 12 are learning in this manner what may be begun ?

A. The first part of the National School Book No. 2.

Q. How is the National School Book, No. 2, that is, the collection of stories of words of one syllable begun?

A. By a repeating lesson from the mouth of the teacher, in the following manner: the teacher says, " The way," class says the same after him; teacher, " of God," class, " of God;" teacher, " is," class the like; teacher, " a good way," class, ditto. Then the assistant, and the boys after him, as before in the cards.

Q. What is done next?

A. The first boy says, " The way;" next, " of God;" next, " is;" next, " a good way." Each child repeating to itself in a whispering or low voice what is said aloud by the child whose turn it is to read.

Q. When the whole class has been exercised in this way, what does the teacher next teach his class?

A. The teacher will make any boy read a whole sentence, or part of it, by pauses, taking particular care to let the voice pause or rest where the sense will admit, besides at the regular stops, thus: " The way—of God —is—a good way."

Q. How long is this continued?

A Till every boy has obtained a slow, clear, and correct mode of reading; and then the lesson may be learnt and read in the usual way, taking particular care to make the due pause at the stops.

Q. What is the way generally in which the first part of the little story-book, No. 2, is then continued to be read?

A. Each lesson or story is read by short portions; and when the whole of any lesson or story has been thus read, it is read afterwards once as it stands in the book, and questions are asked out of it.

Q. How is each child to be taught to read?

A. Slowly, distinctly, and audibly, pronouncing a little louder the last letter of every word, and the last word of every sentence.

Q. How is the quantity which each child reads to be regulated ?

A. It should be a short portion, and each reads in succession till the teacher says, " Next," or points to any particular boy to proceed. · The scholar, who happens to read the last part of the lesson, begins it again ; and thus they go on till the teacher says, " Shut books."

Q. What follows ?

A. The hardest words are spelt off book, and then the next lesson is read over by the scholars, that the teacher may fix its length ; and it is read over and over again, till each child is perfect.

Q. What is a scholar too apt to do, when he meets with a hard word ?

A. To repeat over and over again the easy words which stand before it, till he can stumble upon the difficult word.

Q. How should this error be corrected ?

A. The eye of the scholar should be confined to the single word which puzzles him, by being prevented from pronouncing any other till it be read.

Q. How should he be punished, if he disobeys this rule ?

A. Let the next scholar correct him, and take his place; the best mode of punishing and correcting every error.

Q. How are the spelling words of more than one syllable read, in the National School Book, No. 2 ?

A. The first boy says " Po_" the next " et," the next " Poet," each boy thus taking a syllable, and the third boy in rotation pronouncing the whole word.

Q. When perfect in reading syllabically, the spelling words of more than one syllable, how does the class proceed ?

A. Each boy taking a whole word, 3, 4, or 5 words

compose a lesson; though the length may vary according to the proficiency of the class.

Q. How is the History of Joseph and his Brethren read?

A. By pauses and sentences, thus: Now—Jacob—loved—Joseph—more—than—all his children—because—he was—the son—of his old age—and—he made him—a coat—of many colours.

Q. To what may recourse be had, if distinct and correct pronunciation is lost sight of?

A. To repeating lessons.

Q. What caution should be attended to with respect to the reading the history of Joseph and his brethren?

A. Great care should be taken that no new reading lesson is entered upon, till the spelling lessons which go before, have been read syllabically, and word by word.

Q. Though this book is difficult, what will be the advantage, if it be gone through correctly and perfectly?

A. The scholar may then begin the Sermon on the Mount, or indeed any other reading book with ease and pleasure to himself.

Q. What is the new mode of learning the latter part of the book, No. 2, or words of more than one syllable, by reading and writing at the same time?

A. In the syllabic words, first boy says " po"—all write " po"—next " et," all write " et"—next says " Poet," so on to the end of the lesson; then it is read from the slate (hiding the book) backwards and forwards syllabically, till the teacher gives a signal; then the lesson is read by words, till perfect. Or it may be read by words at once. The slates are next turned, and the words are written by dictation promiscuously, thus: teacher says " poet"— first boy says " po"—next boy says " et" —next " p"—next " o"—next " e"—next " t." The next boy pronounces the word " Poet."—Each letter is written as it is said, and when the whole lesson is thus written, it is read once by words.

Q. What are the books read after the National School Book, No. 2 ?

A. Parables ⎫
   Discourses ⎬ of our Saviour.
          ⎭
   Sermon on the Mount.
   Miracles of our Saviour.
   Ostervald's Abridgement of the Bible.
        Testament.
        Prayer book.
        Bible.

Q. What directions can be given as helps towards enabling the children to read well, and to understand what they read ?

A. In the Book No. 2, the Parables, Discourses, Miracles of our Saviour, and the Sermon on the Mount, the teacher may read the lesson first to the class, if necessary, and the class afterwards by pauses, that is, each child in turn reading the smallest member of a sentence, which contains a distinct idea. This is the first time of going over each book, and the teacher asks the children easy questions out of every lesson. The second time, the children read rather longer passages, according as the sense will admit, the children first questioning one another with the books open, and afterwards, the teacher asking them questions, the books being shut.

Q. Are Ostervald's Abridgement of the Bible, or the Testament, or Bible, read in the same manner ?

A. Not exactly : the teacher does not read the lesson to the class first ; the children take up one another by longer sentences, paragraphs, &c. attending to the course of the narrative, and they at once question one another from each lesson, the teacher continuing to ask them afterwards with the books shut.

Q. What is the new mode of spelling, according to Dr. Bell's Plan called?

A. Unreiterated, because the letters are not repeated over in an useless manner, as was formerly done.

Q. What is the mode of asking the class to spell words?

A. If the scholar reads syllabically, he is also asked syllabically to spell his words thus: faith—ful—ness, which he repeats, faith—ful—ness, and then spells f—a—i—t—h=f—u—l=n—e—s—s, pausing an instant between each letter, and double that time at the end of every syllable.

Q. Should the scholar repeat the syllable as he goes along, or the word after he has done?

A. No. It serves no other purpose than to create delay, and impede his progress.

Q. When the class is expert in this mode of spelling, and in reading by sentences, how is the word asked?

A. In the common way—"faithfulness," but it is always repeated by the scholars by syllables—faith-ful-ness, and what is usually practised now is, a syllable by each boy in turn, and in the spelling, each boy in turn a letter.

Q. What is the advantage of this plan?

A. It tends materially to keep up the attention of the class.

Q. May it not however sometimes be varied?

A. Yes. Sometimes the boy may take a letter only, sometimes a syllable, and sometimes a whole word.

Q. In hearing a class spell, what words does the teacher select?

A. The most difficult, or those which have not occurred frequently, or that may be supposed to be not well remembered.

Q. What quantity may these usually amount to?

A. The number diminishes daily; after a little progress one or two of the hardest words in a lesson will pro-
bably be sufficient, as the rest will have been learnt and
known before.

Q. If the mistake of a letter is made by the scholar in
spelling, how is it corrected?

A. The boy next in order who can set him right, must
only name the single letter, where the mistake was committed, and then he takes his place.

Q. How does the boy, who was corrected, then proceed?

A. He repeats that letter only, and goes on spelling the
rest of the word, subject to the same correction as before
from the boy below him, and he must spell his word
over and over again, if necessary, till he makes no
mistake.

Q. When should the scholar be taught what the accent
means?

A. In beginning to read words of more than one syllable.

Q. What should he be asked respecting it?

A. On what syllable the accent or stress of the voice
should be placed, whether on the first, second, third, &c.
and how the word would be read if placed otherwise.

Q. To what does this lead?

A. Correct pronunciation.

Q. In reading also, what may the judicious teacher instruct his children to do?

A. To lay the stress upon the proper word, and also to
read the smallest member of a sentence, which contains
a distinct idea.

Q. What other mode may be adopted also, for securing
the attention of the children to what they read?

A. Familiar questions being asked by the visitor, the
master, or by the teachers, or even the children themselves,
under the eye and direction of experienced superintendants.

Q. From what period does " Religious Instruction," or learning by heart the Prayers, Graces, Catechisms, &c. commence ?

A. From the period of every child's first coming to the school.

Q. How is this taught ?

A. In small portions at a time from the mouth of the teacher, the class together repeating it after him, at first and then separately, till perfect in each portion as it proceeds.

Q. What is the order in which this Religious Instruction is to be learnt ?

A. First, the Lord's Prayer, then Graces before and after Meat, the second and third Collects of Morning and Evening Prayer, Prayers to be used daily at home, Prayers on entering and leaving Church, the Catechism, and afterwards the same broken into short Questions and Answers.

Q. Is any other explanation of the Catechism learnt ?

A. Yes. Crossman's Introduction, &c. or some other Exposition of the Church Catechism recommended by the Society for promoting Christian Knowledge.

Q. Who are to be considered as monitors of silence ?

A. The teachers of the respective classes.

Q. What should those teachers have who first succeed in reducing their classes to quietness and order ?

A. A double reward.

Q. What punishment should be inflicted on those teachers who transgress themselves, or do not report their scholars who transgress ?

A. They should be deprived of their weekly reward, or even degraded, if necessary.

Q. How is the first offender in this respect to be punished ?

A. His name is noted down, and he is confined, or kept

to the bottom of his class, or any other punishment of this kind, which may occur to the master, till entire silence is obtained.

Q. Is any talking allowed ?

A. No. If any thing is to be said, it must be whispered to the master in a corner of the room; all else is transacted by signs.

Q. Who is responsible for the observation of these rules ?

A. The usher or ushers, who must see that they are duly executed by the teachers.

Q. Still, however, what must be attended to respecting the children in reading ?

A. That each scholar is distinctly heard by his teacher and class fellows. This well managed does not create the insupportable noise too often heard in schools.

Q. What plan may also be adopted for preventing noise when the children go to and from their seats, and enter and leave the school ?

A. Their taking very short steps.

Q. How may the noise, which is occasioned in a numerous school by the words " begin; open or shut books, &c." be prevented ?

A. These and other orders of the same kind are given by signs; such as pointing to the boy who is to begin, raising or falling the hand, or other devices which the teachers are sure to invent or improve.

Q. Can you recapitulate some points to be particularly attended to ?

A. Perfect instruction; the course of study well arranged; due length of lessons; continued occupation; the teachers unceasingly attentive; emulation properly excited; no moment throughout the day lost to any child, but every instant profitably employed; perfect order and regularity in every movement.

Q. How may faults, in a great degree, be prevented ?

A. By never overlooking a single one that may be committed

Q. If however it should be necessary, what are the punishments inflicted?

A. Loss of place or degradation from his class; confinement at extra hours, to recover by diligence what may have been lost by idleness; the same punishment and confinement at extra hours is assigned to those who come late, or absent themselves from school; solitary confinement, imposition, the black book, or register of offences of a serious nature solemnly inspected once a week in presence of the whole school, drawn up in a circle for the purpose, when the nature and consequence of every omission or commission are explained in the language of the school, and the fact tried, and sentence pronounced on the accused by a jury of the best boys, which sentence is inflicted, mitigated, or remitted at the discretion of the superintendant, visitor, or schoolmaster; expulsion or rod only in extreme cases, then by direction of visitors, and every thing done to make a serious and lasting impression.

Q. What is the particular advantage of the Register of Offences, and the manner of inspecting it?

A. It allows time to the accused to make his defence; it produces a fair and open enquiry into the business; it awes by the solemnity with which it should be carried on; it has been experimentally proved to operate as a great preventive of any heinous fault; and above all, gives an opportunity to the visitors to explain to the school at large, the nature of each offence, and to inculcate the best lessons of morality and religion.

Q. What rewards are bestowed?

A. At the weekly examination reward tickets to the teacher, if the progress of the class is satisfactory; and to the two best boys, in each class. Honorary rewards of medals, or books, or clothes at the annual meeting, or annual or quarterly examination ; promotion ; an additional merit ticket occasionally for any particular good conduct. The merit tickets may vary in value, two, three, four, five, or six for a penny. Entering in a fund book the value of the merit tickets, and amount due, and allowing the children to have that amount in a manner, and at a time it will be most useful to them ; giving a little encouragement to those who let their account in the fund book remain without drawing it out for idle purposes.

Q. In building school-rooms, what allowance is generally made for each child ?

A. About six or seven square feet, but the larger the better.

Q. In general are there most boys or girls attend ?

A. In general the former, and therefore the school-room for the girls need not always be so large.

2. What other hints can be given respecting a school-room ?

A. A barn is accounted a model of a school-room ; it only wants windows ; the bottom of which should be about five feet from the floor ; for economy the roof may be without ceiling, walls lime-washed, no plastering, nor whatever can occasion an echo.

Q. Can any general estimate be given respecting the expence of building ?

A. No. It varies so much in different places.

Q. Does the fitting up cost much ?

A. No, but little ; a few forms and a ledge or desk against the 'wall along the sides of the room are most convenient and œconomical, and give the most accommodation within the same space.

Q. What are the principal expenses in establishing and supporting a school ?

A. The building or rent of a room, and the salary of the master or mistress.

Q. Is the cost for books heavy ?

A. No. Under proper regulations, quite inconsiderable.

Q. What are some of the principal mistakes made in schools?

A. Imperfect instruction; not apportioning the length of the lesson to the capacity and proficiency of the scholars; allowing a single scholar to give out, or say the whole, or a greater part of the lesson (especially of short lessons), instead of dividing it into small portions, so as to exercise the whole class in quick succession, and keep alive their attention; not enforcing the due number of lessons; the waste of time by the scholars, when they should be learning their lessons; allowing the classes to sit down too often, which immediately produces inattention; beginning the lesson always with the head boy of the class, and going regularly through the whole; neglecting to unite classes as often as their relative progress will admit.

Q. What other mistakes should also be guarded against?

A. Neglecting due degradation and promotion; quick, indistinct, and low reading; neglecting the due marking of the teachers' books.

Neglecting to teach the classes to move to and from their seats in a regular manner, preserving their due distances, and taking their places in good order.

Disregard to the general rules of the school, and disorderly conduct on the part of the scholars, attended with distressing and deafening noise.

The boy next to the reader not prompting him, if he makes a mistake, till the teacher says, " Tell;" thereby preventing life and energy; or on the contrary, too great eagerness and bawling together.

Neglecting to teach the scholars to read the pages,

chapters, contents of chapters, &c. of a book, and to attend to the points and stops, &c. and sometimes also, on the other hand, permitting them to continue this practice for months after the class is perfect in them.

In the correction of a mistake in spelling, naming more than the letter, and in reading more than the word mistaken.

WRITING.

Q. What is the first process in learning to write?

A. To begin on the sand or on slates with the simplest letter, not quitting it till perfectly learnt; then the next simplest, and so on through the whole alphabet.

Q. What does the scholar next proceed in?

A. Having finished the alphabet by single letters, he writes the whole at once; when those letters, in which he fails, are given him for his daily tasks, till he can write all of them well.

Q. What is the scholar next taught?

A. He is then advanced to write with paper, pen, and ink, on a copy book, the reward of his proficiency.

Q. How is this part of the instruction to be taught?

A. The scholar first writes those letters which are confined within the ruled lines, and then all those which fall below; lastly, all which rise above them, till he is perfect in these respective lessons. The paper is ruled accordingly, so that there may be no waste; or it may be still better to write without lines.

Q. When he can write every letter well, to what is the scholar advanced?

A. To joining hand.

Q. How is the scholar encouraged in his task?

A. His progress is all along marked by his rank on the writing bench; a constant spirit of emulation is thereby kept in action, and his proficiency receives its due reward (which is not a little prized) of precedence and honour.

Q. Should any person be allowed to set a copy, or write a single word or letter in the copy-book for the scholar ?

A. No.

Q. How then does the scholar manage with his copybook ?

A. He has before him his moveable copy either from copper-plate, or prepared by the master, or usher, or teacher, at leisure, on a separate slip of paper, and ready for the whole school in succession. And he is at once taught, by cutting a slip of paper to the width of the lines of his copy, or other device of this sort, to rule his own paper, as before, his slates, which a little practice in this way will soon enable him to do without such helps.

Q. What else should he be taught with respect to writing ?

A. To make his own pen, and do every thing for himself, under the direction, not with the assistance, of the teacher.

ARITHMETIC.

Q. How soon is arithmetic begun

A. As soon as a child enters the school.

Q. In what way ?

A. By learning to count as far as 100, backwards and forwards, and afterwards to repeat the arithmetical tables from the mouth of the teacher.

Q. Will it signify whether the child has learnt his alphabet when he is thus taught to count ?

A. No. It is a relief from his daily task thus to get a small portion of numbers every morning or afternoon.

Q. How are what are termed the ' seven varieties' in figures then taught?

A. Begin by teaching the scholar to read and write any digit by itself, as 7 ; then any number of two places, as 70 and 58 ; then of three places, or a half period, as 400, and 506, and 320, and 637.

Q. Do these seven cases embrace every variety that can occur?

A. Yes, for every number, however long, is composed of a successive repetition of half periods.

Q. Is the scholar then first made perfect in these?

A. Yes. In reading and writing units, tens, and hundreds, or a single half period.

Q. Is any thing now necessary to enable him to read the longest number?

A. No. Because it is only a succession of half periods.

Q. How is this contrived?

A. By dividing every long number into half periods of three places each, reading the right hand figure first, and periods of six places each, by alternate commas and semicolons, placing 1, 2, 3, 4, &c. dots respectively over the figures on the left of each successive semicolon ; thus to read :

73807900048005670000598422007080i
make as follows :

73 ; 807, 900 ; 048, 005 ; 670, 000 ; 598, 420 ; 070, 8o1

Q. How are these divisions then read?

A. Each by itself, as if it was a single half period for previous instruction.

Q. Can you repeat the numbers in this manner?

A. Seventy-three—eight hundred and seven—nine hundred—forty-eight—five—six hundred and seventy—five hundred and ninety-eight—four hundred and twenty—seventy—eight hundred and one.

Q. What is the next process?

A. Pronouncing thousands for each comma, and millions for every dot, thus—seventy-three millions of M. of M. of M. of M. (or quintillions), eight hundred and seven thousand, nine hundred millions of M. of M. of M. (or quartillions), forty-eight thousand and five millions of M. of M. (or trillions) six hundred and seventy thousand millions of M. (or billions), five hundred and ninety-eight thousand four hundred and twenty millions, seventy thousand, eight hundred and one.

Q. What is the advantage of this plan?

A. After this is perfectly learnt, the scholar can note down any given number of figures.

Q. In proceeding to the four first or cardinal rules of arithmetic is the same principle observed?

A. Yes. The elementary parts should be perfectly learnt in classes, by short and easy lessons, repeated as often as necessary.

Q. What should be done before the children learn to add, subtract, multiply, or divide?

A. Care should be taken that every member of the class be able to say the addition, subtraction, multiplication, and division tables, respectively, in any and every way, without the smallest hesitation or mistake.

Q. How is the sum given out?

A. By dictation from the mouth of the teacher, and the whole class set it down without any copy before their eyes, and then read it; and sometimes it is a practice for the boys in the class to give out the sums, by a half period each in turn.

Q. How is the sum worked?

A. The boys take a single step each by turns, correcting and taking places as usual.

Q. When the sum is finished, what is then done?

A. The teacher and assistant passing behind the circle of their scholars inspect the slates, assign his due rank to each performer, and set the scholar, who does not write his sum down correctly and properly, to copy it from one of the best examples till it is well done.

Q. May not two or three classes be employed at the same time in the same arithmetical lesson?

A. Yes.

Q. How is this done?

A. A single voice only being uttered in succession, and all the rest setting down the figure from the mouth of the successive speaker, and each teacher and assistant taking charge of their respective classes.

Q. Are the same rules for classification in arithmetic to be attended to?

A. Yes; In beginning arithmetic, it is expedient to form the class or classes as large as the numbers in the school will admit; also by uniting a superior to an inferior class, the one will bring forward the other, and at the same time improve themselves still more than the others.

Q. What is the order in which the figures are first set down?

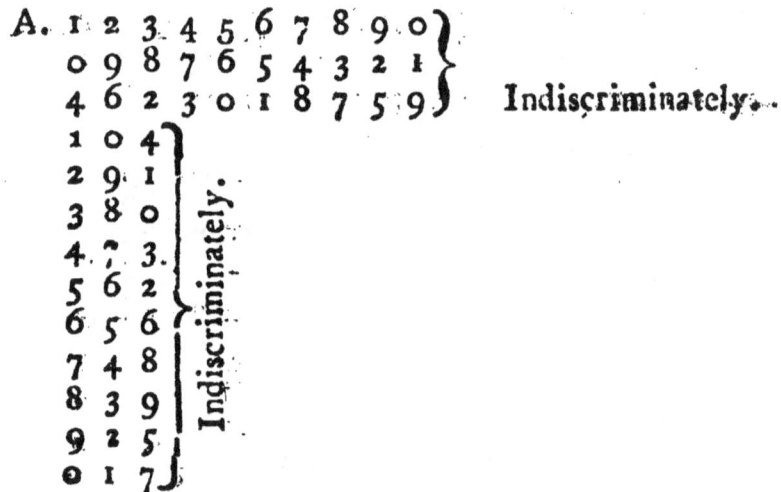

A. 1 2 3 4 5 6 7 8 9 0 ⎫
   0 9 8 7 6 5 4 3 2 1 ⎬
   4 6 2 3 0 1 8 7 5 9 ⎭   Indiscriminately.

1 0 4 ⎫
2 9 1 ⎪
3 8 0 ⎪
4 7 3 ⎪
5 6 2 ⎬ Indiscriminately.
6 5 6 ⎪
7 4 8 ⎪
8 3 9 ⎪
9 2 5 ⎪
0 1 7 ⎭

Specimen of the Admission Book.

No.	Names.	Age.	Parents Names.	Residence.	When admitted.	By whom recommended.	Remarks.	Time of quitting the School.
28	Downer, George.	6	Charles and Ann.	St. John's Parish.	June 2, 1814.	Mr. A. B.	Apprenticed out to —.	
127	Dumper, James.	8	James and Elizabeth.	Middle Brook-Street.	Feb. 9. 1815.	Committee.	Gone to Service at—	

———

Account of Daily Attendance and Absence in each Class, kept on a Slate by the Usher of the School, and suspended in a conspicuous Part of the Room, so as to be seen by the Visitor.

C.	P.	A.	S.	L.	T.	Remarks.
1	19	—	1	1	21	
2	25	1	—	1	27	
3	24	—	3	2	29	
4	28	—	—	—	28	
5	25	1	1	—	27	
	121	2	5	4	132	

C. Class.
P. Present.
S. Sick.
A. Absent without Leave.
L. Absent with Leave.
T. Total.

1st Class		READING.							CYPHERING.						Account of Boys.				REMARKS.
Date 1815.	Day of the Week.	Books.	Ended at Page.	No. of Page.	No. of Lessons.	Repeated Do.	Hours.	Hours in Writing.	Tables, Three-quarters of an Hour.	Rule.	Hours.	Prayers and Religious Instruction, Three-quarters of an Hour.	Examination.	Total Hours.	Boys in School.	Boys Absent.	No. of Teachers.	Total.	
April 17	M	Parables.	23	6¾	11		2	1	Addition. 1 & 9 to 1 and 10.	Addition.	½	Explanation of Words.	½	6	31	6	2	39	Explauntion of Words. ½ an Hour
18	T	Miracles.	3	4¾	9		2	1	1 & 11 to 1 and 12.		1			6	31	6	2	39	Do. ½
19	W		4	¾	8		2	1	2 & 1 to 2 and 2.		1			6	28	9	2	39	Do. ½
20	T		6	1½	11		2	1	2 & 3 to 2 and 4.		1			6	30	7	2	39	Do. ½
21	F								Day of Examination.										
22									Holiday.										
Total				13¼	39		8	4	3		3½	3	½	24	120	28	8	156	2
24	M		7	1¼	7		2	1	2 & 5 to 2 and 6.		1			6	29	5	2	36	Do. ½
25	T.		9	1¼	8		2	1	2 & 7 to 2 and 8.		1			6	29	5	2	36	Do. ½
26	W		10	1¾	9		2	1	& 8 to and 9.		1			6	29	5	2	36	Do. ½
27	T		12	2	11		2	1	& 9 to 2 and 10.		1			6	29	5	2	36	Do. ½
28	F								Day of Examination.										
29	S								Holiday.										
Total				6¼	35		8	4	3		4	3		24	116	20	8	144	2

Names.	M.	Tues.	W.	Thurs.	F.	S.	Total	Rank.	M.	Tues.	W.	Thurs.	F.	S.	Total	Rank.	S.	S.
Bailey, George	2	2	1	1	6		12	1	1	1	3	7	3		15	3		
Bishop, John	33-aa	7	12	10	13		75	14	11	8	7	33-aa	12		71	11	-a	
Bucksey, John	6	6	6	3	3		24	4	12	5	13	5	9		44	6		
Dolten, William	12	18	13	16	19		78	17	18	19	19	14	15		85	20		
Damper, James	33-ss	33-ss	33-ss	33-ss	33-ss		165	30	33-ss	33-ss	33-ss	33-ss	33-ss		165	29	s-s	s-s
Ewens, Peter	5	10	8	9	7		39	6	10	10	5	11	4		40	5		
Freemantle, Hen.	13	15	14	13	11		66	10	9	18	18	6	19		70	10		
Freemantle, Fred.	17	19	10	7	22		75	15	17	15	6	10	13		61	9		
Grant, Thomas	7	13	9	12	2		43	7	6	11	9	9	10		45	7		
Grant, Henry	27	28	26	28	21		130	28	28	26	27	25	26		132	28		
Green, Isaac	8	33-aa	28	27	18		114	24	7	33-aa	12	16	14		82	16		
Gover, William	33-aa	27	27	33-ll	10		130	29	27	27	26	24	27		131	27		
Glass, Henry	21	23	24	17	33-aa		118	26	19	21	20	17	16		93	21		
Harding, Wm.	24	24	23	25	25		121	27	25	25	15	23	25		113	26	-a	
Hughes, Thomas	16	9	18	22	12		77	16	16	12	16	18	11		73	12		
Leggatt, James	14	8	5	8	33-aa		68	11	2	2	1	1	1		7	1		
Lomer, George	22	21	17	14	33-aa		107	20	13	6	21	21	22		83	17		
Mason, George	23	17	21	24	24		109	21	14	20	17	15	18		84	18		
Marner, William	15	5	19	20	15		74	13	21	22	23	3	7		76	13		
Packer, Thomas	18	26	22	18	26		110	23	22	23	14	20	24		103	23		
Prishett, James	19	16	11	11	4		61	9	4	7	8	33-ss	33-ss		85	19	s-s	
Pullen, Henry	3	1	3	4	1		12	2	3	3	2	2	2		12	2		
Rogers, Richard	4	11	7	5	8		35	5	33-ll	33-ll	33-ll	33-ll	33-ll		165	30		
Smith, John	1	3	2	2	5		13	3	5	14	11	19	8		57	8		
South, Thomas	20	12	20	26	16		94	18	26	9	24	22	6		77	14		
Troke, John	25	25	16	23	20		109	22	23	24	25	12	23		107	25		
Turner, Charles	9	4	4	6	9		44	8	8	4	4	4	5		25	4		
West, James	10	14	15	19	14		72	12	20	17	33-aa	13	17		100	22		
West, Henry	26	20	33-a	15	23		117	25	24	16	10	33-aa	21		104	24		

The left-hand **S.** column is labelled **No School.**

A Pasteboard is suspended in the Girls' School Room Winchester, with the following Statement of

Crimes to be punished.

1. Telling lies.
2. Deceit of any kind.
3. Taking God's name in vain.
4. Using bad words.
5. Stealing.
6. Keeping any thing belonging to another.
7. Talking or playing in church or at prayers.
8. Absence from church.

Faults to be punished.

1. Talking or playing in school.
2. Not minding their teachers.
3. Coming to school with dirty hands and face.
4. Coming to school without combing their hair.
5. Staying from school without leave.
6. Not being sorry for their faults.

Merits to be rewarded.

1. Attention at lessons.
2. Attention at work.
3. Being civil to, and minding the teachers.
4. Coming to school with clean hands, face, and hair.
5. Constant at school.
6. Constant at church.
7. Quietest and quickest at work.
8. No mark on the black list for one month.

A

BRIEF SUMMARY

FROM THE

FOREGOING DIRECTIONS.

————

[These Rules may be printed in a separate sheet, and
suspended in the school-room.]

I. The fewer the benches, seats, or desks, the better.
Leave a space for each class to occupy entirely to itself, and
let the children who learn to write succeed each other, one
class at a time, and then very few writing-desks will be re-
quired. Let every class have a clear passage to come out
in order to say its lesson.

II. Short, easy, continued, and perfect lessons.

III. Let the teachers be selected from the higher classes,
but the assistant teacher may be the best boy in each class.

IV. As the whole success of the system depends on a
good selection of teachers, and on their doing their duty,

let the master (or mistress) be as little as possible or never sitting at his desk, but let him see that the teachers, and all their agents under them, are active, and well employed, and let him pay particular attention where his exertions will be most serviceable. As the teachers are good, bad, or indifferent, so will the school be: as the master forms them, so will they form their pupils.

V. A considerable addition will be gained to the number of lessons said in one hour, if they are learnt standing; and if the children should appear fatigued, let them sit down, and copy or write something on their slates; or, go into the play-ground for a few minutes.

VI. Let every thing be done to encourage, to excite emulation; to prevent idleness by finding employment for every moment of the time they are at school, and let not corporal punishment be inflicted, till all other means for correction have failed, and never but by order of the visitors.

VII. Let there be invariably a weekly examination by the visitors and members of the committee.

VIII. Let the Lord's prayer, the graces before and after meat, the 2d and 3d collects of morning and evening prayer, a prayer on entering and on leaving church, short prayers to be used at home, the catechism, &c. be taught by dictation from the teacher in very small portions at a time, and let the children be frequently exercised in the use of them; and when perfect in all of these, the Religious Instruction may be followed by the Catechism broke into short Questions and Answers, and the chief Truths of the Christian Religion may be learnt by heart in very small portions, as well as a larger explanation of the Church Catechism.

IX. Let the books be used in the following order :—
Monosyllabic Cards, called National School-book, No. 1.
first by previous spelling, (see Dr. Bell's Instructions, 6th
edit. page 76.) then word by word.   Do not quit these cards
on any account till the class can read and write the whole
easily, perfectly, and distinctly, and spell every word accu
rately ; the foundation being well laid, renders future progress easy and pleasant.   The words of more than one
syllable in the National School Book, No. 1, first syllabically, then word by word.

National School-book, No. 2.   The few first lessons to be
repeated by pauses, or little rests of the voice, where the
sense will admit, and then gradually by whole sentences,
and lastly, in the usual way, paying proper attention to the
stops, and to the sense and course of the narrative.

Parables
Discourses   } of our Saviour.
Sermon on the Mount.
Miracles of our Saviour.
Ostervald's Abridgement of the Bible.

These books are to be read only in the usual. way, in
small portions at first : the meaning of the words being
asked, and a familiar explanation being given principally
by means of questions and answers.   The whole of these
books indeed should be broken into short questions and
answers, the same as the Catechism Broke, &c.

Testament.
Prayer Book.
Bible.

X. Be very particular about the marked book.   Let it
contain in a blank page the teacher's Christian and sur-
name, the number of the class, the manner in which the class
is reading the book, (whether syllabically, word by word,
or in the usual way) on what day the book was begun in

that manner, and whether 1st or 2d time, &c. of going through it; and let each lesson and the day of the month be also accurately noted down with a pencil in the progress through the book.

XI. Let clear, steady, and distinct pronunciation be constantly observed. Let particular attention be paid to the stops; and if the children are asked occasionally, when one word is harder than another, which is the hardest word in each lesson, and why it is so, it will considerably quicken their attention.

XII. Let quietness, order, and regularity, be invariably preserved, particularly when the children enter and are dismissed from the school.

XIII. The fewer the classes the better. *Equal progress* is the short rule for classification.

XIV. Let nothing imperfectly known be ever passed over, and nothing already well known be dwelt upon.

XV. Let the registers be accurately kept. The daily register for ascertaining individual progress will be a great stimulus to exertion.

XVI. In spelling, take care that the children pause a double length of time between the syllables to what they do between the letters, and let only a single letter, be named when one pupil corrects any mistake of another. The pause between each letter is sometimes continued as long as you would be in counting four at first, till the proper distinctness is obtained.

XVII. If you find any difficulty in getting the scholar

to speak audibly, or to say or do any thing to be said or done, let the scholar so failing forfeit his place to all who can do these things, and he will soon regain his lost honour, and learn to be more correct.

XVIII. Let every scholar be able to tell accurately the number of the page, and the book that he is reading.

XIX. *Mind* these rules before you *mend* them.

N. B. Let the superintendants of schools read with particular attention Dr. Bell's Instructions, 6th edit. chap. x. p. 115, on the mistakes commonly made in schools.

Printed by R. and R. Gilbert, St. John's Square, London.